T 8755

18496

CRAFTY Magic

Nick Huckleberry Beak

Gareth Stevens Publishing
MILWAUKEE

The original publishers would like to thank the following children for modeling for this book: Joshua Ashford, Lana Green, Reece Johnson, Alex Lindblom-Smith, Laura Masters, Laurence Ody, Yemisi Omolewa, Charlie Simpson, and Frankie David Viner. Thanks also to their parents and Walnut Tree Walk Primary School.

The author would like to thank Jonathon for being a brilliant magician and sharing his ideas; Christa, Nic, Kirsten, Paul, and Francis for always being amazed by his tricks (although he thinks they are just being kind); and his brother, Mike — well, because someone has to!

For a free color catalog describing Gareth Stevens' list of high-quality books and multimedia programs, call 1-800-542-2595 (USA) or 1-800-461-9120 (Canada). Gareth Stevens Publishing's Fax: (414) 225-0377.

Library of Congress Cataloging-in-Publication Data

Beak, Nick Huckleberry.
    Crafty magic / by Nick Huckleberry Beak.
        p. cm. — (Crafty kids)
    Includes bibliographical references and index.
    Summary: Describes the equipment and techniques involved in doing magic and provides instructions on how to perform a variety of individual tricks.
    ISBN 0-8368-2481-4 (lib. bdg.)
    1. Magic tricks—Juvenile literature. [1. Magic tricks.] I. Title. II. Series.
GV1548.B42   1999
793.8—dc21   99-22877

This North American edition first published in 1999 by
Gareth Stevens Publishing
1555 North RiverCenter Drive, Suite 201
Milwaukee, WI 53212 USA

Original edition © 1997 by Anness Publishing Limited. First published in 1997 by Lorenz Books, an imprint of Anness Publishing Inc., New York, New York. This U.S. edition © 1999 by Gareth Stevens, Inc. Additional end matter © 1999 by Gareth Stevens, Inc.

Editor: Lyn Coutts
Photographer: Tim Ridley
Designer: Michael R. Carter
Gareth Stevens series editor: Dorothy L. Gibbs
Editorial assistant: Diane Laska

Printed in Mexico

1 2 3 4 5 6 7 8 9 03 02 01 00 99

Introduction

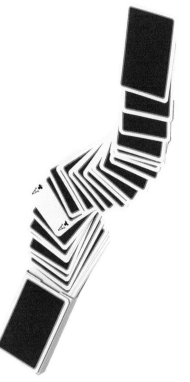

Just saying the word *magic* can make you feel that something wonderful is going to happen — and it will! How do I know this? Because I am a magician, and this book is going to show you how to do some of the best and funniest magic tricks around.

It takes just three things to make a magic show — an audience, a pocketful of good tricks, and YOU! A great magician does not need flashy wands, fluffy bunnies, and expensive magic sets. All you need is enthusiasm and practice. Almost all of the tricks in this book can be done using odds and ends found in your own home.

You will have lots of fun entertaining your friends and family with these magic tricks. But be warned — once you start, your audience will keep asking for more. Happy magic!

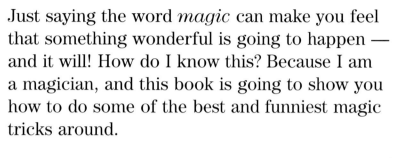

Nick Huckleberry Beak

Contents

GETTING STARTED

MAGIC FUN

Materials

Clock

Cardboard

Paper

CARDBOARD

You will need sheets of thin white and colored cardboard to do the tricks in this book. You can buy large sheets of cardboard at stationery stores, or you can recycle cardboard from containers, such as cereal boxes, and other cardboard packaging materials.

ENVELOPES

You will need a small, 4-inch (10-centimeter) by 8-inch (20-cm), envelope and a large, 8½-inch (22-cm) by 11-inch (28-cm), envelope. The envelopes can be any color.

MARKERS

A marker is a type of felt-tip pen that draws thick lines. If you do not have a marker, use an ordinary felt-tip pen.

PENCIL SHARPENER

All you need is a small pencil sharpener like the one you take to school.

PAPER

You will need a few sheets of white, unlined paper or white drawing paper to do the tricks in this book.

PAPER CLIPS

Any promising magician should have a good collection of paper clips.

PENCILS

You will need an ordinary lead pencil for drawing and a pencil that can be sharpened on both ends for one of the tricks.

WHITE GLUE

This glue is sometimes called wood glue. It is a strong glue that can be used to stick together paper, wood, or even fabric. You can buy it at craft shops and hardware stores.

RECYCLED BOXES

To do the tricks in this book, you will need two empty boxes — one large and one small. A cereal box and a tea box would be ideal. To use a recycled box, flatten it and have an adult cut it along the folds. Be sure that you ask for permission to use these boxes before you empty them.

RULER

A thin wood or plastic ruler with markings for both inches and centimeters is ideal.

Recycled boxes

RUBBER BANDS

You will need large and small rubber bands to do the tricks in this book. You can buy bags of rubber bands in assorted sizes at stationery stores.

TAPE

You will need pieces of clear tape to do some of the tricks in this book.

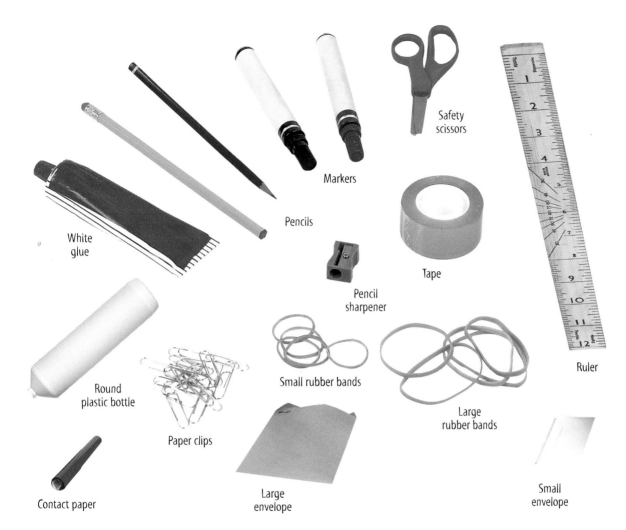

White glue

Pencils

Markers

Safety scissors

Tape

Ruler

Pencil sharpener

Round plastic bottle

Paper clips

Small rubber bands

Large rubber bands

Contact paper

Large envelope

Small envelope

CONTACT PAPER

This adhesive-coated plastic material comes in many colors and designs, and it is usually sold in rolls. You simply peel off the protective paper backing and press it onto a surface or an object. If you cannot find contact paper, you can use leftover wrapping paper and white glue instead.

SAFETY SCISSORS

These scissors are smaller than regular cutting scissors and usually have colored plastic handles. The edges are rounded, so the blades are not as sharp as normal scissors.

CLOCK

You will need a clock or a watch with a second hand.

ROUND PLASTIC BOTTLE

You will need a plastic bottle for one of the tricks in this book. You must have a bottle with straight sides, and it should be about 12 inches (30 cm) tall. The main part of the bottle must be wide enough for a ball to fall through easily. A large shampoo bottle is ideal.

Equipment

Checkers

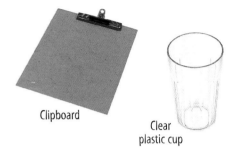

Clipboard

Clear plastic cup

ARTIFICIAL ROSE
You can use a rose made out of either plastic or fabric. You can find one at a craft store or garden center.

FLEXIBLE STRAWS
These plastic drinking straws have small accordion folds near one end that allow the straws to bend. Once bent, they will stay in that position until you move them.

SUPER BALL
This small rubber ball bounces very high when it is dropped.

CLEAR PLASTIC CUP
A disposable drinking cup is ideal, but it must be transparent.

CLIPBOARD
A clipboard holds paper in place when you are writing on it or displaying it. Its hard, flat surface is usually made of wood, metal, or plastic. Paper is clamped under a metal clip at the top of the board.

COINS
You can use real coins or plastic toy money to do the magic tricks in this book.

DETACHABLE PENCIL ERASER
This small eraser fits onto the end of a pencil.

CHECKERS
These round disks come in sets of two colors, usually black and white or black and red. They are made of wood or plastic and are used to play the game called checkers.

THREAD REEL
Inside this small device, a fine thread is attached to a spring-loaded reel. When you pull out the thread and let go of it, the thread is pulled back inside the reel, making an object attached to the thread fly back to its original position. Thread reels are sold at joke and magic shops.

GRAPES
Seedless grapes are the best kind to use for the trick in this book.

HANDKERCHIEFS
You can use large or small cotton handkerchiefs. Brightly colored or patterned ones are best for magic tricks.

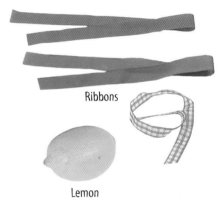

Ribbons

Lemon

HAT
Any sort of hat will do — as long as it is tall and stiff.

LEMON
You can use either a real lemon or a plastic one.

REUSABLE ADHESIVE
This soft, sticky material feels like putty and is often used to stick posters onto walls.

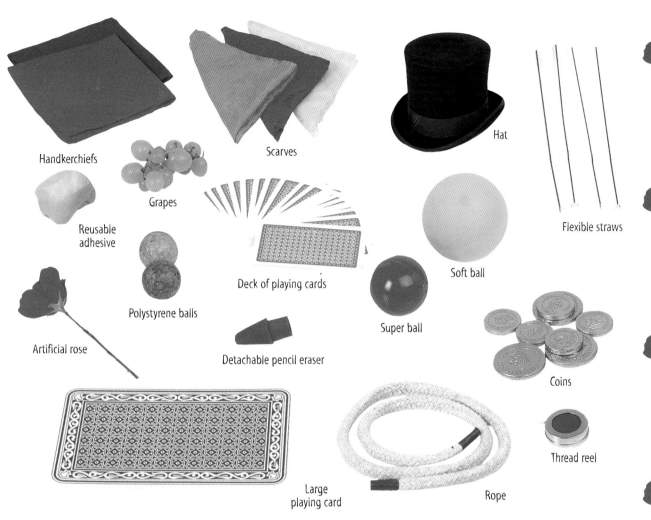

Handkerchiefs

Grapes

Reusable adhesive

Scarves

Hat

Flexible straws

Deck of playing cards

Soft ball

Super ball

Polystyrene balls

Artificial rose

Detachable pencil eraser

Coins

Thread reel

Large playing card

Rope

DECK OF PLAYING CARDS

A deck of playing cards has 52 number and face cards and two jokers. There are four suits, two red and two black, called diamonds, hearts, clubs, and spades. Each suit has numbered cards from ace (one) to ten and 3 face cards, jack, queen, and king. To do the tricks in this book, you will need two decks of cards.

LARGE PLAYING CARD

A large playing card is about four times the size of a normal playing card. You will need two large cards. They are sold at joke shops and toy stores.

BALLS

You will need a soft ball made of sponge or light plastic, as well as small, lightweight polystyrene balls.

SCARVES

Soft, silky scarves in bright colors work best. You will need large and small scarves.

ROPE

You will need two pieces of white cotton rope, a piece 1 yard (1 meter) long and a piece 6 inches (15 cm) long. Wrap the ends with tape to keep them from fraying.

Putting on a Show

To put on a really good magic show, you need to know the three Ps — preparation, presentation, and performance. Forget all that abracadabra mumbo-jumbo. Just remember the three Ps.

PREPARATION

To avoid getting halfway through a really good trick and realizing you are missing a vital piece of equipment, you must be prepared. You must have everything you will need at your fingertips. The only way you can be properly prepared is to make a list of all the items you need for each trick. As you gather these items, cross them off the list. A list is simple to make, and it works. Have you made your list yet? No? Then get to it!

PRESENTATION

How you dress and act in front of your audience is what presentation is all about. Your presentation is very important if you want your magic show to be a great success. To find out more about presentation, read about style on pages 12 and 13.

PERFORMANCE

Congratulations! You have decided to put on a magic show. The first thing you must do is plan your performance. Start planning by selecting the tricks you will do and the order in which you will do them. There are no particular rules to guide you, but, remember, a short show full of fabulous tricks is better than a long show with only a few good tricks.

The best and easiest way to give your magic show atmosphere is to have music playing in the

background. Try to match the speed and mood of the music to the pace and style of your act. If you will be doing a lot of quick tricks, find some fast music. If your show will be spooky and full of shocking surprises, find some creepy music.

If you do not use music, you will have to write a script and rehearse what you are going to say. You might want to introduce each magic trick with a little story, perhaps about where you learned that trick. Whatever you decide to say, be sure you have prepared it. It also never hurts to have a couple of jokes up your sleeve. Jokes can be used to entertain your audience while you prepare your next trick.

Magical Style

Even if you can do some of the hardest magic tricks in the world, your show might flop if your presentation is boring. To be a big hit with an audience you have to have style and pizzazz. The problem is, you cannot buy style and pizzazz at a supermarket. If you try, you will probably come out with two frozen pizzas. Fortunately, presentation style is something you can learn.

DRESS STYLE

The traditional costume for a magician is a stylish suit, a bow tie, and a flashy cape. Today, however, almost any kind of costume is fine. A colorful jacket and a pair of jeans can look just as professional as a fancy suit. If you want to wear your own wacky costume, go ahead. A good rule to go by is — if you feel good, you will look good.

STAGE STYLE

To be a show-stopping performer, you must know the secrets of the trade.

First, always enter from the side or the back of the stage. Walk to the middle, smile at the audience, and wait for the applause. The audience will always clap.

Second, introduce yourself to the audience. You can use your own name or invent a colorful stage name. You might want to make a sign with your name on it and place it beside you on the stage.

Third, always face your audience. Be sure your props and equipment are within easy reach. Your audience did not come to watch you rummage around in a box trying to find the things you need.

Fourth, if something goes wrong, for example, you make a mistake or a trick does not work, try to laugh it off. You can even pretend that the mistake was meant to happen. Then you can do the trick again, but, this time, do it correctly. If you do not know what went wrong, go on to the next trick. After the show, practice the trick until you get it right.

Finally, let the audience know you have finished each trick by taking a small bow. (Save your big bow until the end of the show.) As soon as the audience sees you bow, they will clap and ask for more. Be sure to smile and thank your audience for being so much fun.

ENTERTAINING STYLE

This style is easy to explain. If you have a smile on your face and look like you are enjoying what you are doing, the audience members will enjoy themselves, too. Try to look confident and relaxed. When you talk to your audience, speak out loud and clear. No one will hear your great jokes if you mumble and mutter.

PROFESSIONAL STYLE

If the audience asks you to repeat a trick, refuse politely. A trick is never as good the second time around. Move on to your next trick and tell the audience "this one is even better"!

Magicians are always asked to show how a trick works, but never be tempted to give away the secrets of your magical craft. If you tell your secrets, you will have to learn a whole new routine.

Topsy-turvy Pencil

Are you ready to do your first magic trick? Great! This trick is very easy to do and will totally bamboozle your audience. The knack is to perform the trick quickly so your audience does not have time to figure out how you did it. Sometimes magicians have to be sneaky. This trick should be performed only once.

YOU WILL NEED
- Pencil (without an eraser at one end)
- Pencil sharpener
- Detachable pencil eraser

1. Sharpen the blunt ends of the pencil with the pencil sharpener. Make sure that both ends of the pencil look the same.

2. Put the detachable pencil eraser on one end of the pencil. Your pencil should look like an ordinary pencil, but you will know that it is not.

3 Hold the pencil in your left hand so the eraser is hidden. Make sure you have a firm hold on the eraser. Point to the sharpened end of the pencil with your right hand and say, "This is a very strange pencil." Try to make your voice sound mysterious.

4 Place your right hand around the pointed end of the pencil and pull the pencil away from your left hand. The eraser must stay hidden in your left hand. Curl the fingers of your left hand to make a tunnel. Draw the audience's attention to the pointed end of the pencil and say, "The pointed end of this pencil has magically moved to the other end!"

5 Push the pencil into the tunnel you have made with your left hand. Make sure the pencil slides into the eraser. Keep pushing the pencil until it comes out the other side of the tunnel. Say to the audience, "Now look what has happened. The point has moved and there is an eraser on the other end of the pencil." Is that spooky, or what?

Runaway Ribbon

You are probably wondering what makes this piece of ribbon so special. Just wait and see. This trick will impress you as much as it does your audience. Runaway Ribbon is an excellent opening trick for a magic show. It is easy to do, and you can invite a member of the audience to assist you on stage.

YOU WILL NEED
- Pencil
- Ribbon

1 Hold the pencil so the audience can see it clearly. Hang the ribbon over the pencil. Make sure the end of the ribbon closest to you is the longest. In a moment, you will see why this is important.

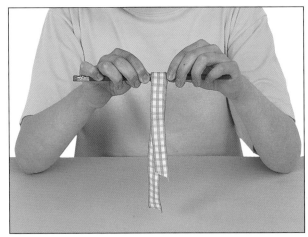

2 Place one finger gently on the edge of the ribbon where it lies over the pencil. Start turning the pencil toward yourself so the ribbon winds around the pencil.

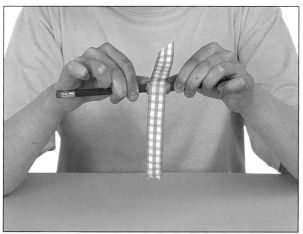

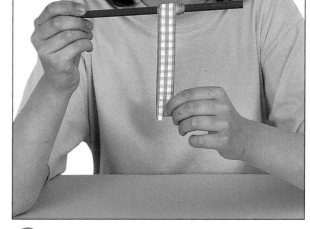

3 When most of the ribbon has been wound onto the pencil, the shorter end of the ribbon will suddenly roll over the top of the pencil. As soon as this happens, STOP turning the pencil. You must practice this part of the trick to get your timing perfect.

4 A piece of ribbon should now be hanging from the pencil, as shown. The rest of the ribbon will look as if it is wound around the pencil. Hold the pencil with one hand and the two ends of the ribbon with the other. Now get ready to impress the audience.

5 Pull the ribbon slowly to add suspense. Continue pulling it until there is no ribbon on the pencil. Wow! The ribbon has melted right through the pencil. Make sure the audience can see that the ribbon has not been cut. After this trick, your reputation as a great magician will spread far and wide.

HANDY HINT

You can invite a member of the audience to assist you with this trick. It will be his or her job to hold the pencil while you pull the ribbon.

Hanky Pranky

This magic trick is a favorite. To make the pencil look as if it is going through the handkerchief, all you have to do is create a secret gap between the handkerchief and your hand. Practice your sleight of hand in front of a mirror until it is so slick that you almost fool yourself.

YOU WILL NEED
- Handkerchief
- Pencil

1 Curl the fingers of your left hand to make a tunnel. Position your hand so the tunnel runs up and down and lay the handkerchief over it.

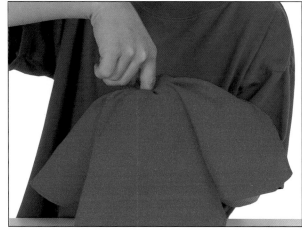

2 Push the handkerchief just slightly into the tunnel, using the forefinger of your right hand. Do not move your finger just yet.

3 Use the middle finger of your right hand to push one edge of the handkerchief into the tunnel. You might have to open your left hand a little to do this. The audience must not see you making this gap between the handkerchief and your hand.

4 Now pull your fingers out of the handkerchief. Pick up the pencil with your right hand and push it into the gap between the handkerchief and your left hand. Continue pushing the pencil until the pointed end can be seen coming out from under the handkerchief.

5 Lay the pencil on the table and hold the handkerchief open so the audience can see that there is no hole in it. All you have to do now is enjoy the applause.

Magic Knot

Here is your first trick using a piece of rope. There is a knack to pulling the scarf off the rope for the big finale, so you will need to practice this trick quite a few times before you perform it in front of your family and friends. This trick is easier to do if you use a small, silky scarf.

YOU WILL NEED
- Piece of rope, 1 yard (1 m) long
- Small soft scarf or handkerchief

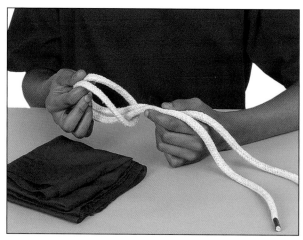

1 Fold the rope in half. Place your right hand about halfway along the rope to hold the rope still. Pick up the loop in your left hand and fold it over your right hand. Keep your right hand in the same position. Place the loop over the ends of the rope and thread the ends through the loop. Pull gently to close the loop a little. The rope must not be twisted or crossed.

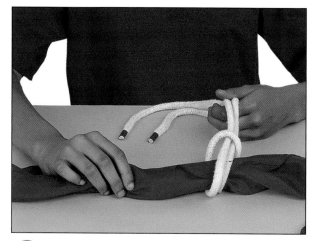

2 Lay the rope with its loop on the table. Fold the scarf or handkerchief in half, diagonally. Continue folding until the scarf is narrow enough to fit easily through the loop. Thread the scarf through the loop. Gently pull on the ends of the rope to close the loop around the center of the scarf. Do not pull the rope very tight and try not to twist it.

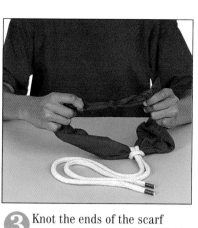

3 Knot the ends of the scarf together to form a circle. Hold up the scarf and the rope to show the audience the knots that lock the scarf on the rope.

4 Hold the rope with both hands and pull on the ends of it. The loop will disappear, leaving the rope perfectly straight.

5 Ask a friend to hold both ends of the rope. Look at where the scarf is knotted to the rope, find the part of the knot parallel to the rope, and hold that part with two fingers.

6 Pull firmly on the scarf. Wow! You have pulled the scarf off the rope without cutting the rope or untying the other knot. That is what your audience will call magic!

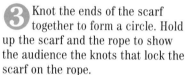

21

Slippery Knot

This trick will take a lot of practice. You have to be able to make the false knot without a hitch. Read these instructions carefully so you know exactly how to hold the rope. To make sure your audience never catches a glimpse of the knotted rope in your right hand, keep the back of that hand facing the audience.

YOU WILL NEED

- 6 inches (15 cm) of rope with a knot in the middle
- Piece of rope, 1 yard (1 m) long

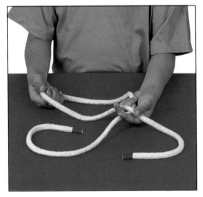

1 Hide the knotted rope in your right hand. Lay the long rope on the table and make a loop. Hold the rope in your left hand, as shown. Your thumb should be placed firmly over the point where the rope crosses itself. Your third and fourth fingers should be inside the loop. The end of the lower section of rope should pass between your first and second fingers.

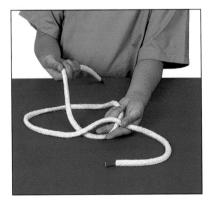

2 Use your right hand to thread the end of the lower rope into the loop. It must pass under the rope that forms the loop, as shown. Move your third finger so it squeezes the upper rope against your second finger. Keep firm pressure on the rope with the fingers of the left hand while the rope is being pulled by the right hand.

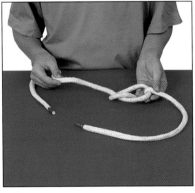

3 Before the knot gets too tight, slide your third finger under the rope that is being pulled. (This will take lots of practice.) Keep hold of the rope between your thumb and forefinger. Your second and fourth fingers can be moved out of the way. Keep pulling on the rope so it closes around your third finger. Then carefully pull out your third finger.

4 Keep holding the rope between your thumb and forefinger. Keep the knotted rope in your right hand hidden from the audience.

5 Close your right hand around the long piece of rope just above the knot and slide it down the rope. As your hand passes over the false knot in the long rope, the knot will disappear. Slide your hand all the way to the bottom of the rope.

6 When your right hand reaches the bottom of the rope, pretend to pull the knot off the rope. Throw the knot you have been hiding in your hand to the audience. They will be very impressed.

HANDY HINT

To make it easy to conceal the piece of knotted rope, tie the knot as small as possible. Then trim away any excess rope from both sides of the knot.

Wacky Knots

This two-part rope trick shows you how to tie a knot in a piece of rope without letting go of the ends and how to tie a knot using only one hand. When you have mastered these knots, challenge your friends to copy your feats of dexterity. You are bound to have some chuckles as your friends tie themselves up in nutty knots.

YOU WILL NEED
• Piece of rope, 1 yard (1m) long

1 **Wacky knot number 1:** Lay the rope on the table and fold your arms, as shown. One hand should be tucked under one arm, the other hand should be resting on top of the other arm.

2 Without uncrossing your arms, pick up one end of the rope with each hand. You will have to lean over the table so your hands can reach the ends of the rope.

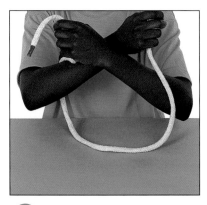

3 When you have twisted and squirmed enough to pick up the ends of the rope, start to uncross your arms. Do not uncross them too fast, or the rope will snag, and you will have to start from the beginning.

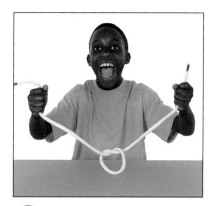

④ When your arms are uncrossed, you will see that you have made a knot in the rope. If you do not have a knot, then you did not cross your arms correctly. Try again!

⑤ **Wacky knot number 2:**
To make a knot using only one hand, hold the rope so it passes first between your thumb and forefinger, then your third and fourth fingers.

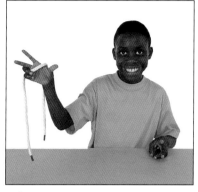

⑥ Tightly curl your third and fourth fingers over the rope. Make sure they are holding the rope firmly. Open your first and second fingers like a pair of scissors.

⑦ Flick your wrist so the end of the rope nearest you falls over the back of your hand. Reach down with your scissor fingers and take hold of this shorter end of the rope. Let go of the rope you are holding with your third and fourth fingers.

⑧ Lower your hand so your fingers point downward. Jiggle your hand so the rope over the back of it falls forward. As the rope passes the short end held between your scissor fingers, it will form a knot.

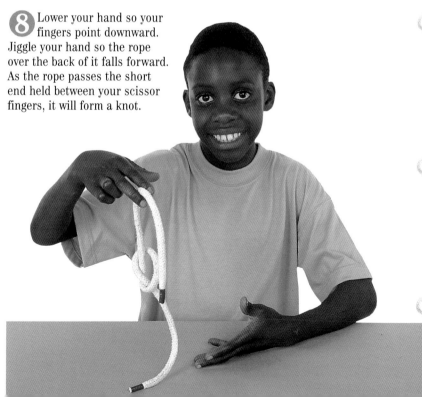

Where is the Coin?

You will see magicians perform this trick on stage or on television. It involves sleight of hand and more than a little bit of sneakiness. You must convince the audience that the coin is in the cup by making sure they hear it fall into the cup. Is the coin in the cup? No way!

YOU WILL NEED
- Large scarf or handkerchief
- Coin
- Clear plastic cup

1 Hold your right hand with your fingers pointing upward. Place the middle of the scarf or handkerchief over your hand. Position the coin on the scarf so you can grip it with the fingers of your right hand.

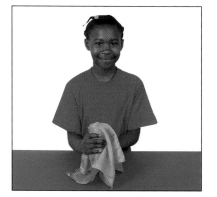

2 Hold the cup in your left hand. Place the scarf upside down over the cup so the scarf hides the cup and the coin. Let go of the coin. It will make a sound as though it has fallen into the cup. What really happens is this . . .

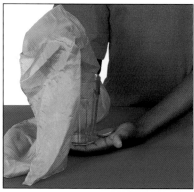

3 Tilt the cup away from you when you cover it with the scarf, so when you let go of the coin, it does not fall into the cup. Instead, the coin drops onto the side of the cup and makes a noise, but it falls into your left hand. Double sneaky!

④ Now hold the scarf-covered cup in your right hand. Use the forefinger of your left hand (remember that the coin is hidden in this hand) to make a dip in the middle of the scarf. You can invite someone from the audience to do this.

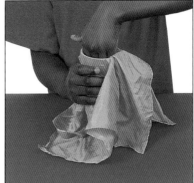

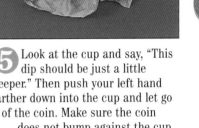
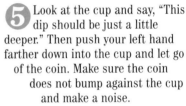

⑤ Look at the cup and say, "This dip should be just a little deeper." Then push your left hand farther down into the cup and let go of the coin. Make sure the coin does not bump against the cup and make a noise.

⑥ Bring your left hand out of the cup and gently pull the front of the scarf downward. As you do, the coin will rise to the top of the cup. You can also pull the scarf quickly, so the coin literally jumps out of the cup. Whichever way you do it, this trick is always a real treat.

HANDY HINT

Hiding a coin in your hand is called palming. To palm the coin swiftly and secretly takes skill. Practice in front of a mirror until you can fool yourself.

27

Handful of Coins

Handful of Coins might seem like an easy trick to do, but it takes time and effort to make every gesture totally convincing. This trick is another one you should practice in front of a mirror. When you think you have mastered it, perform it for a friend before you include it in your magic show.

YOU WILL NEED
• Large pile of coins

1 Place the pile of coins on the table in front of you. Lay your hands, palms down, on the table.

2 Pretend to pick up a coin with your right hand. Your movements must be convincing.

28

3 Place the nonexistent coin in the center of your left hand. Look carefully at the picture above to see how you should position your hands and fingers.

4 Form a fist with your left hand. Point to your left fist with the forefinger of your right hand. Tell the audience you are going to make the coin disappear.

5 Open your left hand to show the audience that the coin has vanished into thin air. If you do not think your audience will be fooled by this trick, just try it and see.

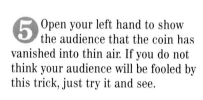

29

Quick Separation

This game really tests your hand and eye coordination. The goal is to separate a stack of checkers into two piles in the shortest possible time. After you have practiced this trick, challenge your friends to a game of Quick Separation. You will need to have someone be the timekeeper. Good luck!

YOU WILL NEED
- 4 black checkers
- 4 white or red checkers
- Ruler
- Clock or watch with a second hand

1 Stack the checkers one on top of the other, alternating black and white. Challenge your friends to separate the stack into a black pile and a white pile in the shortest possible time. No matter how quick they are, you will be quicker.

2 Here is how you will do it. Hold the ruler flat on the table and slide it under the stack of checkers. Then quickly flick the ruler from side to side. The black pieces will go to one side, and the white pieces will go to the other side.

3 Checkers will fly everywhere if your technique is not right. If you flick the ruler too slowly, the stack will fall over. If you flick the ruler too hard or too quickly, two or three pieces will fly off at the same time. The only way to get it right is to practice.

4 How many seconds did it take you to make two separate piles of black and white checkers? If you did it in less than 10 seconds, you are doing very well. You could try doing it with more than eight checkers, but it is quite difficult. The stack has a tendency to fall over all by itself. Crash!

HANDY HINT

If you want to make this game more challenging, increase the number of checkers in the stack. But be warned — the taller the stack, the easier it is to knock over.

Keep It Under Your Hat

This is one of the silliest tricks around. Do not be surprised if your friends groan when you say you are going to do it. There is no need to practice this trick, but it is important to make a big show of muttering magical words and waving your hands over the hat. If you think you are an actor, here is your chance to prove it.

YOU WILL NEED
- Hat
- Clear plastic cup containing something to drink

1 Ask a friend if he or she would like to watch you try a fantastic new magic trick using a hat and a cup of something to drink.

2 Carefully place the hat over the cup. Tell your friend that you are going to drink the contents of the cup without touching the hat.

3 Say some magical words and wave your hands over the hat. Then announce that you have done the trick. Your friend will not believe you.

4 Your friend will probably lift up the hat to see what has happened. If not, invite him or her to look under the hat.

5 As your friend lifts up the hat, quickly grab the cup and enjoy the drink. See, you did not have to touch the hat to get to the cup!

Hovering Ball

This stunt is not so much a trick as it is a challenge. You have to get a small ball to hover in the air above the end of a straw. It sounds easy, but it actually takes a lot of patience to get the stream of air just right to hold the ball up. If you are willing to huff and puff for the sake of scientific discovery, this challenge is for you!

YOU WILL NEED
- 2 flexible straws
- 2 small polystyrene balls

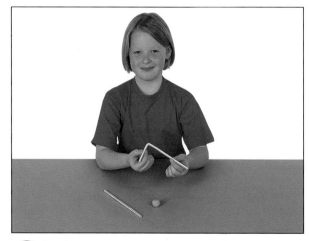

1 Bend the straw to form a right angle. Your family and friends will have no idea what is going to happen next.

2 Place the straw in your mouth and hold the ball just over the end. Start to blow a steady stream of air through the straw.

③ Let go of the ball and see how long you can keep it hovering in the stream of air coming out of the end of the straw. If you blow too hard, the ball will shoot up quickly, then fall to the ground. The ball will hover longer if the stream of air is soft but even.

④ When you think you are pretty good at this, it is time to make the challenge extra hard — two straws and two balls. Use the same technique as before, but you will need to huff and puff a little more. If "Daredevil" is your middle name, why not try three straws and three balls?

The Big Card Trick

You may have seen this trick performed many times. Now you will be able to do it yourself. You can choose any number or suit for the large playing card, but a card of the same number and suit must be at the top of your deck of playing cards. The two cards attached to the large card must be smaller numbers than the large card.

YOU WILL NEED
- Reusable adhesive
- Deck of playing cards
- Large playing card
- Large envelope

1 To prepare for this trick, use a small piece of reusable adhesive to attach a two and a four of any suit onto the back of the large ten of clubs card. Place the cards in the envelope. Be sure that the ten of clubs is the top card on your deck of cards. Now let the show begin.

2 Invite a guest from the audience to join you on stage. Ask your guest to cut the deck of cards. To cut the cards, all your guest has to do is take a pile of cards off the top of the pack and lay them down beside the remaining part of the deck.

3 Place the bottom half of the deck at a right angle across the top of the cut cards. Positioning the cards this way will show you where the deck was cut and where you will find the ten of clubs. Tell your guest that he or she will shortly see his or her secret card.

4 Remove the top cards from the pile and turn over the next card. Without looking at the card, show it to your guest. Tell him or her it is very important to remember this secret card.

5 Now ask your guest to shuffle the cards as much as he or she likes. When the cards are shuffled, put them into the envelope that contains the large card attached to the two smaller cards.

6 Tell your guest that you are going to find his or her secret card. Pull the two card out of the envelope. Ask if this is the secret card. Your guest will say no. Then ask, "Is it bigger than this?"

7 Reach into the envelope again. This time, pull out the four card. Repeat the routine in step 6. Now is your big moment to astound and amuse everyone. Put your hand back into the envelope and pull out the large ten of clubs card. Show it to your guest and say, "Is this big enough?" You have shown your guest that you knew the chosen card was the ten of clubs all the time.

HANDY HINT
You can make your own large playing card with stiff white cardboard and a black felt-tip marker. It does not matter what card you choose to draw, as long as it is the same as the top card on your deck of cards.

Predict-a-Card

This card trick is one of the cleverest. Your friends will not be able to figure out why the chosen card is always the red ace. They might try to outwit you, but they will never succeed. To make this trick work, you have to arrange the cards in a special order and learn the secret method of counting them.

YOU WILL NEED
- 5 playing cards of either black suit, numbered 2, 3, 4, 5, and 6
- 1 ace playing card of either red suit

1 To prepare for this trick, you have to arrange the six cards in a particular order. The top two cards must be black and the third card must be the red ace. The bottom three cards are all black. To lay out the cards, deal them from left to right so the red ace will be the third card from the left.

2 Now it is show time! Lay out the cards as explained in step 1 but lay them out facedown. Remember to start on the left. Ask a guest from the audience to think of his or her favorite number between one and six. It does not matter what number he or she chooses, because you are a magician.

3 The goal of this trick is to show that, whatever number your guest selects, the chosen card will always be the red ace. If the number is three, count three cards from the left and push that card forward.

4 Turn over the other five cards to show that they are all black. Turn over the chosen card to reveal that it is the only red card. Wow! Do not repeat the trick, just leave the audience guessing.

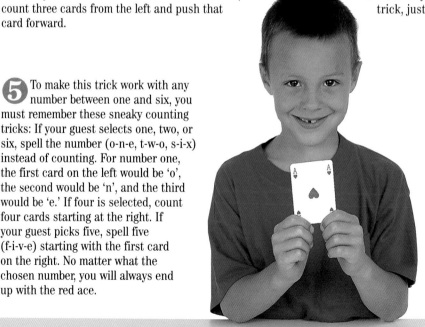

5 To make this trick work with any number between one and six, you must remember these sneaky counting tricks: If your guest selects one, two, or six, spell the number (o-n-e, t-w-o, s-i-x) instead of counting. For number one, the first card on the left would be 'o', the second would be 'n', and the third would be 'e.' If four is selected, count four cards starting at the right. If your guest picks five, spell five (f-i-v-e) starting with the first card on the right. No matter what the chosen number, you will always end up with the red ace.

Card Cascade

This card trick is one that will surely make your audience groan. As soon as they see all the cards unfold, they will know they have been conned. Sometimes magicians just have to be super crafty! To make the Card Cascade, use an old but complete deck of playing cards. Once the cascade is made, the cards cannot be used for anything else.

YOU WILL NEED
- Deck of playing cards
- Tape
- Large playing card
- White glue

1 Divide the deck of cards into the four suits. Remove the jacks, queens, kings, and jokers. Choose one suit and arrange the cards in numerical order from ace (one) to ten. Tape the cards together end to end, as shown.

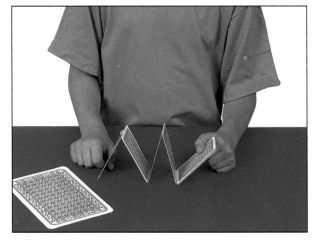

2 Fold up the long line of taped cards, accordion-style. The cards should form a neat, flat pile. If they do not, carefully retape any cards that are crooked or overlapping.

3 Glue the back of the ace along the right-hand edge of the large playing card. Repeat steps 2 and 3 for the remaining three suits of cards. When gluing the playing cards to the large card, alternate the colors and overlap the edges. If you are careful making the Card Cascade, you will have a trick you can use again and again.

4 Hold up the large card with its back facing the audience. Keep a firm grip on the folded cards. You do not want them cascading down at the wrong moment. Ask a member of the audience to name a card of any suit between ace (one) and ten. Tell the audience you are holding that very card in your hand, right now. Turn the large card around and let the cards unfold. Point to the chosen card.

Magic Box

The Magic Box can produce objects out of thin air. One minute the box is empty, the next minute it is not. Only you know how the secret box can hold a lemon, a pack of cards — or even an elephant. But if you want to pull an elephant out of the box, perhaps this trick should be called the Magic Trunk!

YOU WILL NEED

- Small recycled box
- Large recycled box
- Tape
- Scissors
- Marker
- Ruler
- White glue
- Contact paper
- Lemon

1 To make the Magic Box, tape the ends of both boxes closed. Cut the top off the small box and draw a line along one long and two short edges of the large box.

2 Carefully cut along the lines you have drawn to make a hinged lid on the large box. Be sure that both boxes are empty before you start making the Magic Box.

3 Make a hinged lid on the other side of the large box, too, but with the hinge on the opposite edge. You must make these lids correctly or your box will not be very magical.

4 Tape or glue the small box securely to the inside of one of the hinged lids on the large box. The open top of the small box must face the hinge on that lid.

5 Cover the box, inside and out, with contact paper and cut two strips of contact paper to make tabs. Stick one strip onto the outside edge of each lid, fold it in half, and stick it to the same edge, but inside. Now put the lemon in the small box.

6 You are ready to make magic! Place the box on the table with the lid containing the lemon on the bottom and its tab facing you. Hold both tabs and prepare to open the box.

7 As you raise the Magic Box, pull on the tabs, letting the audience see your face through the hole. Say to the audience, "See, this box is empty — but not for long."

8 Carefully close the box and put it back onto the table with the lid containing the lemon on the bottom. Turn the box around so the tab facing you is on the top lid. Hold that tab to lift the lid. Remove the lemon from the small box with a great flourish and show it to the audience.

Tricky Tubes

Tricky Tubes is another classic trick used by magicians everywhere. It involves moving a handkerchief from one tube to another, while giving the impression that both tubes are empty. At the end of this trick, you stun the audience by pulling a handkerchief out of the empty tubes. To make this magical miracle, you need only cardboard, paper clips, a rubber band, and a handkerchief.

YOU WILL NEED
- 2 12-inch (30-cm) squares of different colored cardboard
- 9 paper clips
- Rubber band
- Small handkerchief

1 Steps 1, 2, and 3 show you how to prepare for this trick. Roll the two pieces of cardboard to make two tubes. Make one tube narrower than the other so it will fit inside the larger tube. Use four paper clips on each tube to hold it together.

2 What makes this trick work is an ordinary paper clip. Unfold the paper clip to have hooks at both ends, as shown. Attach a rubber band to one hook. Then roll up the handkerchief and thread it through the rubber band.

3 Hook the other end of the paper clip over the top edge of the narrow tube, with the rubber band and the handkerchief on the inside of the tube. Make sure the handkerchief is completely hidden inside the tube.

4 Now it is time for the show! Hold up the large tube so the audience can see that it is empty. This should not be difficult, because the tube really is empty!

5 Now pick up the narrow tube and slide it down into the large tube. As it slides through, the hook holding the handkerchief will catch on the top edge of the large tube.

6 Pull the narrow tube out from the bottom of the large tube. Hold up the narrow tube to prove to your audience that it is empty.

7 Put the narrow tube on the table and slide the large tube over the narrow tube. The handkerchief will fall inside the narrow tube. Say to your audience, "From two empty tubes, I will pull out a handkerchief." Then pull the handkerchief out of the narrow tube.

Half and Half

Half and half is the only trick in this book that involves cutting something into pieces, but you will not be sawing anything — or anyone — in half. You will start with something simple — a playing card and a piece of ribbon. The sneaky thing about this trick is that you never, ever, cut the ribbon.

YOU WILL NEED
- Playing card
- Smooth, shiny ribbon
- Safety scissors

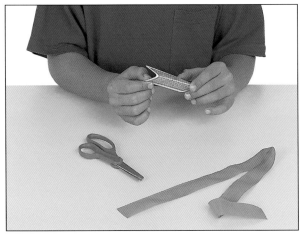

1 Fold the playing card in half, lengthwise. Run your finger over the fold to flatten it.

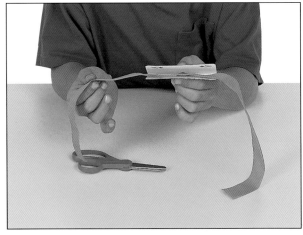

2 Lay the ribbon inside the folded card, with the ends of the ribbon hanging out of the card on both sides.

It is important that you use safety scissors for this trick. Safety scissors have rounded blades that are not very sharp. If you use sharp scissors, this trick will not work.

3 Hold the card and ribbon in one hand. Use the safety scissors to cut across the center of the card and the ribbon. Always cut across the folded edge first.

4 Your audience will not believe their eyes. The safety scissors has cut the card in two, but the ribbon is still in one piece. How does this trick work? It just does!

47

Joke in the Mail

Want to send someone a shocking surprise? All it takes is paper, paper clips, rubber bands, and tape. Joke in the Mail is so easy to put together that you could make one for each of your friends. Of course, they might not still be your friends after you play this joke on them. Always be careful when you bend paper clips. The wire ends are sharp.

YOU WILL NEED
- Paper or thin cardboard
- 3 paper clips
- Tape
- 2 small rubber bands
- Small envelope
- Marker

1 Fold the paper or thin cardboard into thirds. Press the folds flat, then unfold the paper.

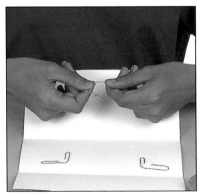

2 Bend two paper clips to make L-shapes, as shown. Bend a third paper clip into a circle.

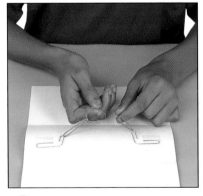

3 Tape the L-shaped paper clips to the middle third of the paper. Loop rubber bands around the ends, as shown, then thread the rubber bands onto the wire circle.

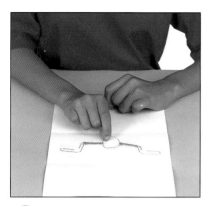

4 Slowly turn the wire circle around and around. The rubber bands will twist and tighten. Whatever you do, do not let go!

5 Fold the paper without letting go of the wire circle. Put the folded paper into the envelope and seal the envelope securely.

6 Use the marker to address the envelope, then mail or deliver the envelope to a friend. Boy, is your friend in for a surprise!

7 When your friend opens the envelope and removes the paper, the rubber bands will rapidly unwind, causing the wire circle to make a loud noise as it rubs against the paper. This trick is bound to give your friend a good laugh.

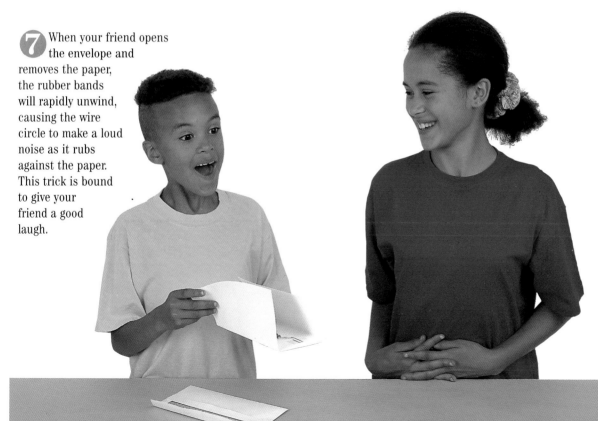

Gobble the Grape

Just when you thought these tricks could not get any sillier, here is the all-time famous grape trick! To do this trick well, you have to be able to pretend you are holding a grape when, in fact, your hand is empty. This trick definitely requires practice, especially just before your show.

YOU WILL NEED
• 2 small seedless grapes

① Carefully place one of the grapes in your mouth, without your audience seeing you do it. It is crucial that the audience thinks you have only one grape.

② To begin this trick, pick up the remaining grape in your right hand. Show the grape to the audience, then pretend to place the grape in your left hand.

3 Form a loose fist with your left hand to hide the grape that really is not there. Point to your left hand with the forefinger of your right hand. Try not to talk during this trick. The grape might pop out of your mouth!

4 Put your left hand on the top of your head and pretend to squash the grape. Spreading your fingers as you press down makes it look as though you really have squashed the grape.

5 Open your mouth to show the audience the grape inside it. If you did this joke convincingly, the audience will think the grape has moved through your head and into your mouth. Pretend to take the grape out of your mouth with your right hand. Then hold out your right hand and show the audience the grape that has been there since the beginning of the trick. Now you can do the trick all over again.

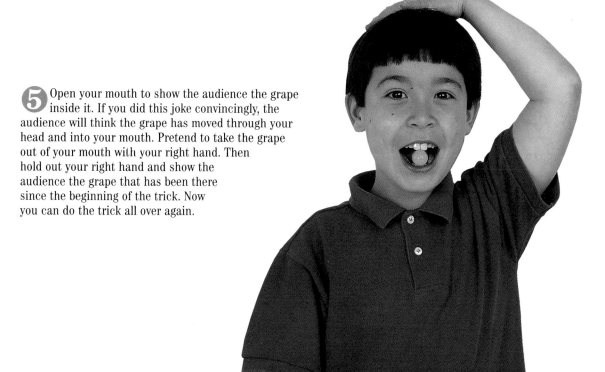

Mental Magic

In this trick, you are going to read a person's mind. You will not find out his or her deepest secrets, but you will discover that person's chosen number. You must promise never, ever, to reveal the magical secret of this mind-reading trick to anyone.

YOU WILL NEED
- Paper
- Clipboard
- Ruler
- Marker

HANDY HINT
You can do this trick in different ways. You can draw magic symbols around the numbers, then pretend to be deep in concentration, or you can ask two or three friends to think of numbers at the same time.

1	2	4	8
7	6	13	10
5	3	15	14
3	15	7	13
11	7	6	15
9	10	5	12
13	14	12	11
15	11	14	9

① Clamp the paper to the clipboard. With the ruler, draw three lines down the paper to make four columns. Copy the numbers in the picture on page 52 into the columns. Copy the numbers exactly. If you get them wrong, you will not be reading anybody's anything!

② Ask a friend to think of a number between 1 and 15. Be sure to tell your friend to keep the number a secret. Then, ask if the secret number is in column one. Remember your friend's answer and ask again for each of the other three columns. Some numbers are repeated, so your friend's number could be in more than one column.

③ Without even looking at the columns of numbers, you will be able to guess your friend's secret number immediately. Here is how you do it. Memorize the number at the top of each column (1, 2, 4, and 8). After you find out in which columns the secret number appears, you simply add the numbers at the tops of those columns. For example, if your friend's number appears in the last three columns, just add 2 plus 4 plus 8. Your friend's secret number is 14. Mental Magic is so easy!

Bouncing Hanky

This quick trick will give your audience a laugh. It works because no one expects the handkerchief to go zooming into outer space. The Bouncing Hanky trick is even funnier if you try to look as surprised as your audience. Before you do this trick, be sure to move all breakable objects a safe distance away.

YOU WILL NEED
- Large handkerchief
- Super ball
- Rubber band

1 To prepare for this trick, open the handkerchief and place the ball in the center of it.

2 Wind the rubber band around the handkerchief, just under the ball, to hold the ball in place.

3 In the middle of your magic show, take the prepared handkerchief out of your pocket and pretend to blow your nose. Make funny noises to get a laugh.

4 Hold the handkerchief so the audience cannot see the ball. When you take the handkerchief away from your nose, drop it onto the table or the floor.

5 Wow! Look at that! Your handkerchief is going where no other handkerchief has gone before! Bouncing Hanky is a good trick to have in your pocket — or up your sleeve — to add humor to your show.

Returning Rose

To make this joke work, you have to have a fall guy. A fall guy is the person on whom the joke is played. To get a fall guy, you might offer a friend the rose you are wearing, as a gift for helping you perform a trick. Do not, however, expect your friend to thank you for the rose after you play this joke on him or her.

YOU WILL NEED
- Thread reel
- Artificial rose
- Scissors

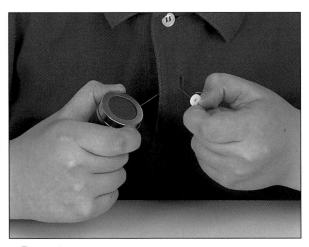

1 To do this trick, you must wear a shirt or jacket with buttons and buttonholes. The thread reel should be on the inside of your shirt or jacket, out of sight of the audience. Pull the line inside the thread reel through an open buttonhole.

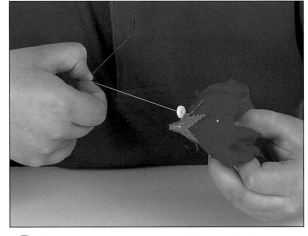

2 Have an adult cut the stem off the artificial rose, just below where the flower and the stem meet. Securely tie the end of the thread reel line to the rose. If the line is not tied tightly, the rose will fall off when the thread reel springs into action.

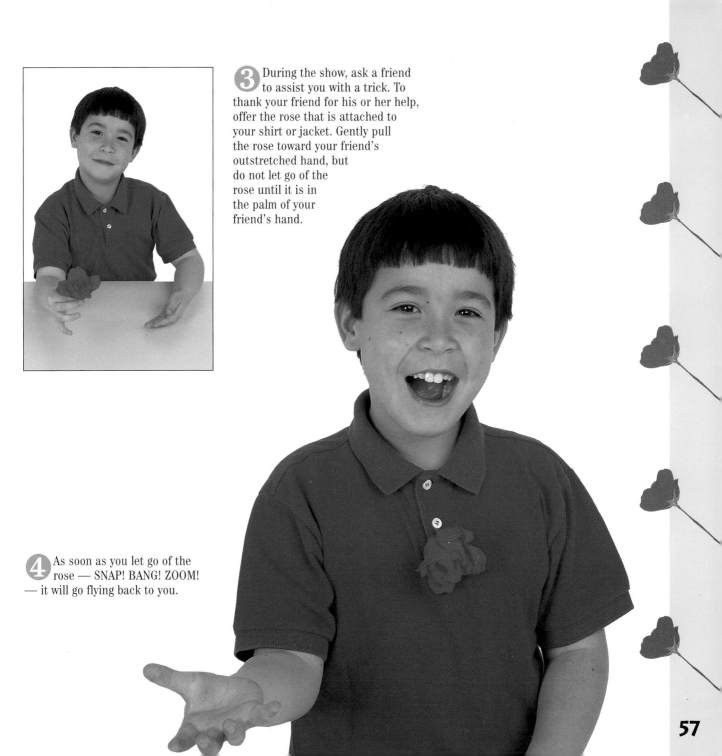

3 During the show, ask a friend to assist you with a trick. To thank your friend for his or her help, offer the rose that is attached to your shirt or jacket. Gently pull the rose toward your friend's outstretched hand, but do not let go of the rose until it is in the palm of your friend's hand.

4 As soon as you let go of the rose — SNAP! BANG! ZOOM! — it will go flying back to you.

Bottomless Tube

This trick is a good way to get people's attention. To make the Bottomless Tube, all you need is an empty plastic bottle. There is, however, one catch to this trick. The ball you use must be only slightly smaller than the width of the bottle to be sure it will not slip through.

YOU WILL NEED
- Round plastic bottle
- Scissors
- Soft ball

1 To prepare for this trick, have an adult cut the top and bottom off the plastic bottle to make a tube. Be sure the bottle you are using is empty and has been cleaned out. Decorate the tube if you want to.

2 Now, let the show begin! Hold the tube up so the audience can see that it is empty. Then, hold the ball above the tube, as shown. Get ready to drop the ball into the tube.

3 When you drop the ball into the tube, quickly move your hand to the bottom of the tube so you can catch the ball as it comes out. You have to be quick; the ball will not wait for you.

4 Repeat this routine until your audience starts to yawn. The next time you drop the ball into the tube, squeeze the tube gently so the ball cannot fall through it. Suddenly, your audience will wake up. Where is the ball? Try to look perplexed as you peer into the tube. Then give the tube a shake. Just as you are about to give up the search for the ball, stop squeezing the tube and let the ball fall out.

5 Sometimes, you might want to pretend not to notice that the ball is missing. Just keep doing the dropping and catching routine until someone in the audience shouts, "The ball is gone!" Then stop squeezing the tube and let the ball drop out. Doing the trick this way might not sound very funny, but it usually gets a laugh.

Farewell Finale

Sadly, it is time to go. The curtains are coming down on the greatest magic show on Earth. So, say goodbye to your audience in a magical way with this special finale. When you do this trick, follow, very carefully, the instructions for folding the paper. If you fold the paper the wrong way, you will end up saying goodbye to yourself.

YOU WILL NEED
- 2 pieces of paper
- Marker
- Scissors
- White glue

1 To prepare for this trick, place one piece of paper with a long side toward you. Draw a large picture of someone waving on the paper. Keep the picture simple because you will have to draw it again later.

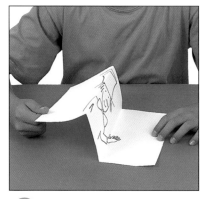

2 Turn the paper so the picture is upside down. Then fold the paper in thirds, accordion-style, making the right-hand section slightly larger than the other two. The right-hand section should be on the bottom, as shown.

3 Now, fold the paper in half, away from yourself, making the top half slightly smaller than the bottom half. While these instructions might sound complicated, you should find that the folding is really very easy.

 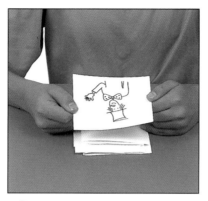 

4 Cut a rectangle out of the other sheet of paper. It should be exactly the same size as the bottom half of the folded paper. Draw the same picture on the rectangle that you drew on the folded paper.

5 Glue your small picture to the front of the larger half of the folded paper. Put the bottom of the picture closest to the fold. Apply glue carefully so it does not spread onto other sections of the folded paper.

6 Hold the paper with the fold at the bottom and the small picture facing the audience. To keep the paper from unfolding, support the back section with your index fingers. Get ready for your big finale!

7 Tell the audience you are going to give them a big farewell wave. Then, quickly pull the paper sideways, unfolding the back section to reveal the large picture. Before their very eyes, the audience will have seen the tiny farewell wave become a great big farewell wave.

Glossary

astound: to impress or amaze with surprise or wonder.

bamboozle: to fool or trick in sneaky or dishonest ways.

cascade: a small waterfall with a very steep drop or a quantity of some material that falls or drops quickly like a waterfall.

conned: used dishonest and sly tricks to gain someone's trust and confidence in order to cheat them or steal from them in some way.

crucial: absolutely necessary to achieve a particular result; essential.

dexterity: physical or mental skill and quickness, especially in using the hands.

feats: remarkable stunts or actions that require great skill, strength, or courage.

finale: the last, and usually most impressive, part of a performance.

flick: a quick, sharp movement, such as a stroke with the fingertip or a snap of the wrist.

flourish: a sweeping or waving motion, especially with the arms, that is usually overdone.

forefinger: the first finger, or index finger; the finger closest to the thumb.

fraying: pulling apart, separating, or weakening, usually due to rubbing, the threads or fibers of cloth or other woven materials.

gesture: a physical movement, especially with the arms or hands, that expresses or emphasizes a particular feeling or idea.

impression: the effect or image that a person's looks, words, or actions produce on the mind or emotions of another person.

knack: a special skill, talent, or ability to do something that is tricky or complicated.

palming: holding an object in the palm of the hand in such a way that the hand looks empty.

perplexed: confused or uncertain; puzzled.

pizzazz: an exciting kind of attractiveness or liveliness; colorful and showy style.

sleight of hand: skillful or clever movement of the hands to fool someone or create a false impression; skillful use of the hands to perform a magic trick.

stunt: a usually difficult, and sometimes dangerous, action performed to get attention, show off a skill, or cause a thrill.

thread: (v) to guide some kind of long, thin material, such as thread, string, yarn, or wire, through a small or narrow opening.

topsy-turvey: turned upside down or in a confused or disorderly state.

tuck: to push an edge or a loose end of an object inside or under another object.

More Books To Read

10 Awesome Card Tricks. John Railing (Troll)

50 Nifty Super Magic Tricks. Shawn McMaster (Lowell House)

The Blackstone Family Magic Shoppe (series). Gay and Harry Blackstone (Ideals Children's Books)

Fun Files: Magic. Linda Stephenson (DK Publishing)

Henry Gordon's Magic Show. Henry Gordon (Scholastic)

Houdini's Greatest Tricks. Monica Kulling (Random House)

Magic Funstation. Patrick Page (Price Stern Sloan)

Magic Step-by-Step. Tom Russell (Sterling)

The Most Excellent Book of How to Be a Magician. The Most Excellent Book of How to Do Card Tricks. How to Present Your Act (series). Peter Eldin (Copper Beech Books)

Videos

Bob McAllister's Amazing Magic. (Lightyear Entertainment)

Fun Magic: With Items Found Around the House. (Video Specialties)

Magic of Illusion: Ropes & Coins. (Paperback Video)

Quick Tricks: Fun 'n Easy Magic (Best Film & Video)

The Rainy Day Magic Show. (Library Video Company)

You Can Do Magic: Easy as 1-2-3. (Lowder, Bark Productions)

Web Sites

www.angelfire.com/pe/SimpleMagik/

www.conjuror.com/magictricks/free_tricks1.html

Due to the dynamic nature of the Internet, some web sites stay current longer than others. To find additional web sites, use a reliable search engine with one or more of the following keywords: *card tricks, coin tricks, conjuring, Houdini, illusions, magic, magicians,* and *sleight of hand.*

Index